GIRL
TALK

GIRL
TALK

LUCIENNE PICKERING

GEOFFREY
CHAPMAN

ALSO AVAILABLE:

Boy Talk
Parents Listen

Geoffrey Chapman
An imprint of Cassell
Wellington House, 125 Strand, London WC2R 0BB, England

First published as *Girls Talk* 1981.
Reprinted with corrections 1986.
Second edition first published as *Girl Talk* 1992.
Reprinted 1993, 1994, 1996

British Library Cataloguing-in-Publication Data
A catalogue record for this book is available from the British Library.

ISBN 0-225-66675-8

The illustrations on page 62 are based on illustrations in Gordon Bourne, *Pregnancy* (Cassell, 1984) and used by permission.

Typeset by Fakenham Photosetting Ltd, Fakenham, Norfolk, NR21 8NL
Printed and bound in Great Britain by Hillman Printers (Frome) Ltd, Somerset

For you,
for today
and tomorrow

FRIDAY

I've decided to be an author when I grow up, so I am going to record all the most interesting events in my life, in this book. I shall call it 'Kate's Diary'. I shan't bother with every day because most days are the same, just going to school—and that's not worth writing about, except sometimes like today.

In history this afternoon, Pete asked me to marry him! He wrote it on a piece of paper and passed it to me and I was just going to answer when Miss J. looked up, so I lent him my felt pens instead.

I told Mum at tea-time and she laughed and said she thought eleven was a bit young to think about marriage, and we had a whole lot of growing up to do before then. Sometimes I feel as though I can't wait to be grown-up, and then other times it scares me, and I'm glad I've still got Mum and Dad to live with. Anyway, I was quite pleased about Pete, that he liked me, I mean. I felt happy all evening.

This being happy is a funny thing. It keeps changing. For instance, when I was young, I can remember how happy I was just thinking about my birthday. All the night before I lay awake thinking of the present I wanted. Then when I had it, after a while, it just became one of my toys. I liked it still, but it had lost the 'happiness' thing.

Sometimes I do a job for mum and she gives me that special look, all warm and just-between-us, and I feel so happy I could burst.

Now there is another kind. When I'm asked to do something I really don't want to do, a whole battle goes on inside me. I think up all sorts of reasons why I shouldn't, and why it's unfair. You have no idea how hard it is to swallow down my feelings and give in. But when I do, everyone smiles at me and I'm walking on air. Is that what happiness is?

SATURDAY

I helped Dad wash the car. I'm not really all that virtuous, but I'm hoping he'll give me some extra pocket money to put towards a Walkman.

It occurs to me, as I write this, that I am much more honest to my diary than I am to other people. I don't want everyone to know what I think, but I like saying it to someone like this book. I wonder what would happen if we told the truth all the time to our friends? Would they still be our friends? I'll have to think about that some time.

While I was helping Dad, I asked him what he thought about this happiness business, whether it's just having what you want, or doing what you don't want to do. He says it's more a question of giving than getting, like the pleasure you have watching someone open a present you have given them. He also thinks it is something that goes on in your mind —an attitude, a way that you live your life. He thinks you must learn how to enjoy little things.

'Look at the almond blossom,' he said. 'Doesn't that make you feel good?' It was just showing pink in the bud and I felt a little thrill of excitement that comes with spring and the promise of something to come. I took a photo of it with my instant camera just so that I would remember this day.

The end of all that talk was, Dad forgot about his car and I was left to polish it on my own.

SUNDAY

It has rained all day and everyone got into a mood. It began when I put the television on to watch a film and Neil came in to put on a record. I turned up the television and he turned up the stereo, I shouted at him, he thumped me, I kicked him, then Mum and Dad arrived. We both got told off and everything else got turned off.

Dad said Neil shouldn't hit girls even if it was his sister. Mum said I ought to have more self-control being eldest. I hate being the eldest, so much is expected of you.

I went off in a huff to my room, but Mum followed me up and sat on my bed in that sort of way which says 'we haven't finished talking about this'.

She asked me if I had noticed how irritable I was with Neil lately. I said he was just a stupid little boy—I was still feeling pretty mad about it all. Mum said he was not all that much younger than me, it was just that I am growing up rather fast at the moment, and getting impatient with things that make me feel childish.

She says it is important to have self-control when you grow up. Otherwise your body and your feelings take over and tell you what to do even when your mind tells you that it is wrong to do it.

That's a bit difficult to work out but I suppose it means that when I was kicking Neil, I knew all the time that it was wrong, but I couldn't stop. But as I thought this I knew it wasn't true—I didn't want to stop. I must have made a choice.

Well, that's all right, I'm a free agent, why shouldn't I make my own decisions about what I do? The only thing is—there's only me to blame if it's wrong! Well, if that's independence I'm glad I'm not grown up yet. Mum and Dad can go on telling me what to do. But that's not what I want either. I don't know—it's all very complicated.

My uncle made a drawing of Neil and me on holiday two years ago. I'm sticking it in the book, on the next page, just to remind me of how we were before all this growing up began.

GROWING AND CHANGING

What is really happening to Kate is that she is changing and growing all at the same time. This is a time when all kinds of changes begin in a young girl's life.

Not only is the body preparing itself for the future when she may become a wife and mother, but her feelings and attitudes will also change and mature so that she is able to love and care for people as a wife and mother, instead of being as a child with her parents.

All this takes time, as Kate's mother told her; it happens slowly over the next few years. If you read this book you will see how Kate discovers these changes in herself and learns a lot about life as well.

As you follow Kate through this book you will need to be sure of the facts about yourself and your body, how it works and how it grows. Kate's mother has told her quite a lot already as she was growing up.

I expect your mother or father has told you some of the things you want to know about yourself, and about babies— and about boys.

You may also have learnt some things at school. Some schools have films to show juniors, about life and growth and birth. Then of course there is the talk among your friends which is another way of sharing knowledge.

With so many ways of finding out things, it is a good idea to have a book in which the facts are all collected up and put into some kind of order. Then if you have any doubts about anything at all, or if you don't believe or don't agree with what your friends say, you can look it up in this book and know that you can believe what is written here.

SOME FACTS TO START WITH

First of all I want you to look back at the drawing of Kate and Neil. You will see how alike they are. Not only do they have a family resemblance, but there is not much difference in their shape and size. Kate is only a bit taller than Neil, and has the same slim body without any 'womanly' shape.

The family resemblance is something we all have in common with our parents and their parents. You will read some more about this farther on in the book.

At the moment we are considering the changes that have begun in Kate and also in you, if you are about the same age.

The changes are very real, not imagined or guessed at by adults. There are actual physical and chemical things going on inside you which cause the changes. It is no use thinking that it won't happen if you ignore it, and go on behaving like a child.

You have absolutely no control over this change, it is as certain as the mechanism in an alarm clock. It is set to begin at a certain time: nobody knows *exactly* when, only *about* when. But we do know quite a lot about *how*.

If you can learn about the changes before they all happen, it will be easier for you to understand yourself and how you are behaving. This is a big step forward in growing up.

When you hear adults talking about 'immature' people or 'immature' behaviour they are talking about people who cannot behave in a responsible way. Perhaps when you are arguing with your brother or sister, your parents say 'Oh do grow up, you two.' They are asking you to become mature and responsible.

You can see, from the way Kate's parents talk about things with her, that they are very anxious for her to grow into a mature and caring person. Your parents and others who care for you want this too, or they would not have bothered giving you this book to read and keep.

At this moment you are still a young girl, but in the next few years you will grow into a young woman.

You can see below a diagram of the inside of a woman showing all the parts that are concerned with having babies—these parts are sometimes called sex organs. I expect you will see them called that in your biology books in school.

We use diagrams a lot for learning about how things work. A photo does not show parts clearly enough and cannot show inside anything. When people buy a piece of equipment like a food processor or a sewing machine or a car, they are always given a handbook with diagrams all carefully labelled and showing how it works. If something goes wrong an expert in that particular machine will say exactly which part is not working and you will know and understand because you have the diagram and the book to look at.

You are, without doubt, a most carefully designed and

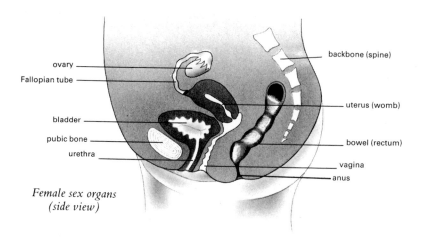

Female sex organs
(side view)

intricately made human machine and that is why you need to look carefully at this diagram and try to remember some of the names. They are strange words for you to learn and come from foreign languages like Latin and Greek. You will probably not use them very often in your lifetime but it is a good thing to know how to say them and to understand what they are if someone else says them. Once you understand what they mean, you will not need to look them up. You will also come to recognise your own body messages and will understand a doctor if he or she says any part of your body needs medical care.

Look at each word in italics, read what is said about the part, and then find it in the diagram.

Ovary The little 'factory' in which thousands of tiny eggs are made. The eggs are called 'ova': one egg is an 'ovum'.

Fallopian tube The 'road' along which each separate ovum (egg) will travel to the womb.

There are two ovaries and two Fallopian tubes.

Uterus Usually called the 'womb'. Normally, the ovum simply dies and disintegrates in the womb. But if the ovum is fertilised it does not die: it begins a new life that will become a baby. Then it stays in the womb and the womb will be the home for the new life for about nine months, until the baby is born. You will read more further on in this book about how the ovum is fertilised and how the new life grows in the womb.

Vagina The passage leading from the womb to the outside of the body. It is the pathway that everything must use coming from the womb to the outside world.

You can see from the picture on page 14 where these parts fit into your body. You cannot feel them because they are placed safely in the framework of your backbone and hip bones. The only part you can feel is the vagina because it is

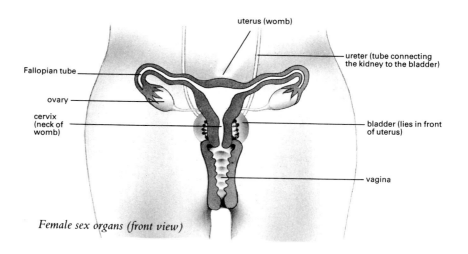

Female sex organs (front view)

just between your legs and behind the opening through which you pass water (the urethra).

If you watch a mother with her children you will see how she embraces them, holds them close to her, protects them. In the same way the new baby, before birth, is sheltered and protected within the mother.

It is this closeness of a baby and its mother right from the start of its life that creates the bond between parents and children. It is necessary, for babies need to feel loved and wanted and safe.

A loving father shares this closeness as much as he possibly can, even before the birth of the baby, by loving and holding the mother in his arms, by protecting her from hurt and by loving the tiny new life that grows in her.

THIS WORD 'SEX'

This love of a man and a woman for each other is called sexual love. These are words you have probably heard quite often: sex, sexual, sexuality. Being a man and being a woman are separate activities and feelings, and yet they are also complementary. They go together. They are made purposefully,

to be together, to make a pair, to fulfil themselves. A man makes a woman feel 'womanly' and a woman makes a man feel 'manly'. This is what is meant by their sexuality.

Little children are not aware of their sexuality because the sexual glands have not begun their work. Little boys do not feel different playing with boys or with girls. They are not really noticing themselves because there is so much exploring to do outside themselves. They are busy finding out about everything.

By the time you are reading this book, you will have gained a great deal of knowledge about people and things. You are gradually becoming more interested in yourself. This period of learning about yourself is called adolescence. It lasts quite a few years and because it happens when we are thir*teen*, four*teen*, and upwards, you may be referred to as a 'teenager'.

= 2 =

WEDNESDAY

Science—the usual boredom disappeared when Mrs Adams produced her wall charts of the human body! Even the back row sat up. She said, 'We are going to learn about glands and how they work' and straight away we all sank back into our heaps of boredom. Then she said, 'In particular the sexual glands' and everyone sat up again. I'm sure I saw her hide a smile ...

THE SEXUAL GLANDS AND HOW THEY WORK

In the last chapter we mentioned the actual physical and chemical changes which take place at this time of your life. These changes are brought about by the work of certain special glands.

You will learn all about the different kinds of glands in your body when you do human biology at school. We have quite a number of them and they are very important. They all have their special functions: for instance, glands cause tears to come into your eyes. There are others that produce the saliva that keeps our mouths moist and enables us to swallow—if you have had a sore throat you will know how the glands swell and become painful.

What interests us here are the sexual glands. These are the ones which begin to work in adolescence, change you into a young woman, and, one day, make it possible for you to have babies.

You have already identified these in the diagram of the female sexual organs. They are called 'ovaries' and there are two of them, one on each side of the womb.

These two ovaries have two jobs to do. They release chemicals which are absorbed by the bloodstream and so are circulated all through the body; they also produce the ova, or 'life-cells' for making new life, and send them on their journey to the womb.

The chemicals they produce are called 'oestrogen' and 'progesterone'. They are both hormones and do different things for you.

Oestrogen, carried by the blood to all parts of your body, gives you your 'femininity'. That is to say it affects the way you talk and walk, the shape of your figure, the growth of your hair, the softness of your skin—all those special characteristics that mark you as different from a man.

Progesterone is more directly to do with the womb and the preparation of it for the purpose of housing a baby and giving a baby all it needs before birth.

THE JOURNEY OF THE OVA AND 'PERIODS'

I mentioned earlier that you have a kind of built-in alarm clock which is set for the time you will begin your changes.

In each person the setting is different. This 'alarm clock' is really another gland called the pituitary gland, which is at the base of your head. Its job is to send messages to the various parts of your body that are concerned with having babies. In the biology books these parts are called 'the reproductive system'.

We are not able to feel any of these glands working in us, just as we cannot 'feel' our nails or hair growing or our blood circulating, but it all happens just the same. It is the special study of doctors and scientists over many years that has given us all this knowledge about ourselves.

We do have some proof that these things are taking place and this is what is explained in this section. In every adolescent girl becoming a woman there is a monthly 'ovulation'. This means that once in each month one of the ovaries will release a ripe ovum (egg) into the Fallopian tube nearest to the ovary. Its journey will begin.

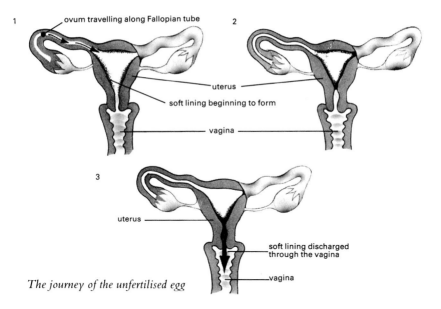

The journey of the unfertilised egg

In the pictures you will see that it is the left-hand ovary and tube that is working, while the right-hand one remains inactive.

If the ovum (egg) meets any sperm to fertilise it, it becomes a living cell capable of growing into a baby: you will read more about this later on in this book. Otherwise (and usually) the ovum dies within twelve hours; it disintegrates and is absorbed by the Fallopian tube.

While the ovum is on its way, the womb is also busy growing a soft lining to its walls (see the diagram). This soft lining is like the making of a nest to house a baby. If the ovum becomes fertilised the new life can then be bedded into the lining of the womb and fed and cared for until birth, but of course normally the lining is not required for this purpose.

So what happens to the lining of the womb? Well, because it has no further use, it has to be sent out of the womb. The blood which is part of the lining becomes thin and the lining detaches itself from the womb and trickles out through the vagina.

When this happens it is called a 'period'—doctors call it 'menstruation', which comes from the Latin word for 'month'. When you see signs of bleeding on your pants or toilet paper, you will know the 'period' has begun. You will put a small, suitable sanitary pad inside your pants, to protect your clothes and absorb the blood.

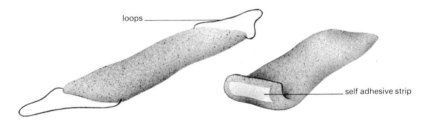

loops

self adhesive strip

The first time this happens to you you must tell your mother who will give you your sanitary pads (sometimes called 'towels') and explain how you wear them. Some have loops and you attach them to a belt, and some have a strip of adhesive on the back which just fixes the pad to the inside of your underpants. If you cannot tell your mother, perhaps you have an older sister or a good friend who is older than you. Your father also knows all about this and you may be happier talking to him about it—you must decide for yourself who makes you feel comfortable and easy when talking about these matters.

It could happen, of course, when you are in school, in which case you will find a woman teacher you are 'at home' with — normally your form tutor — and tell her what has happened. She will take you to the rest room and fix you up with a pad. She will not mind you telling her — many girls have done so before and after all she is a woman like you and understands.

Generally speaking the first period is a very small one and only a few drops of blood show, so that if you do notice in school you could probably wait until you are home before telling anyone. Many young girls who talk to their mothers about these things before they happen prefer to carry a little sanitary pad wrapped in a clean polythene bag, at the bottom of their school bag. That way they are always prepared and do not worry about when it will start.

You do not feel the lining detach itself from the womb — the bleeding has nothing to do with the kind of bleeding that happens from a wound — it is not a hurtful thing, just a normal happening in every woman who is able some day to have a baby, if she chooses.

The loss of the blood will last for three to five, or maybe seven, days; it is different for everyone and you will soon get used to your own cycle. Your 'cycle' is just another word for the pattern of your monthly ovulation and period.

The first few periods are not only small ones, but they may not be very regular. Several months may go by between one and the next. It is just part of the developing of the sexual organs, which are finding their 'rhythm'. It is nothing to be worried about, but if you do become anxious then it is best to talk to your doctor. Remember also about the 'clock': every girl has a different starting time, some as early as ten years old and some as late as fifteen.

Mothers and fathers are quite proud of their young daughters when they become old enough to start periods. It is a step forward into the adult world: you join the grown-ups and share with them a little of the mystery of life.

Whilst all these things are happening inside you, there will be changes in your body that are much more visible to you. You will begin to grow breasts and develop a slim waistline, and your hips will broaden a little so that you have 'curves'. Women's magazines spend a great deal of time discussing

'figures', how to keep them and how to reduce them! You will have to be content for a little while just to let your figure grow and develop naturally. It is very harmful to try 'slimming' when you are normally growing, unless your doctor has arranged this for special medical reasons.

Another development you will see is the growth of hair around the vagina and under the armpits. This is called pubic hair.

With the growth of hair comes an increase in the working of the sweat glands. You will perspire more under the arms and around the neck and forehead.

All these signs and changes will begin soon for you, if they have not started already. When they do, you will know that you are really 'growing up' and preparing for all the excitements, pleasures and mysteries of loving and living a full and happy life as a woman.

— 3 —

SATURDAY

This summer, we are all going on holiday together. Mum and Dad, Neil and myself, and Sarah and Jim and the children.

Sarah is Mum's youngest sister, she's more our age than Dad and Mum, so we don't call her 'Aunty'. She and Jim are married (I was a bridesmaid) and they have a boy called Simon and a little girl called Emma.

Sarah is going to have another baby some time round Christmas so Mum thought it would be a good idea if we all spent a holiday together, so Sarah can get some rest while we all help with the children.

I love looking after Simon and Emma, they both talk a lot and are really good fun. I expect that's because their parents are very friendly and talk all the time to them.

I really admire Sarah a lot. I wouldn't tell her that, but she's just what I'd like to be. She's always interested in you and listens to you, and doesn't make you feel young or silly.

She's even like that with her children, she talks to them like little grown-ups and answers everything they say seriously.

Jim is like that too. He has a lot of patience, he shows Simon how to do everything he wants to do and lets him try out things for himself. Everyone likes them and they have lots of friends.

That's another thing, I don't seem to be much good at keeping friends at the moment. Either they change or I do, but either way we keep changing!

I'm going to stay with Sarah in the half-term holiday, all on my own, and help her look after the children. I'm looking forward to that; we have great talks about all sorts of things. I'm glad she's having a baby. I didn't take much notice when the other two were born, but somehow it has all become more interesting to me now. They said it's because I'm going to be godmother to this baby, but I don't think it's just that. Somehow I feel more grown-up about this baby. The other two were like having more children in the family for me to play with. I was one of them. Now I feel more like one of the grown-ups—as though in a few years it could be me having a baby. I want to share everything with Sarah about this baby.

ON HOLIDAY

Most afternoons Sarah has a rest and Jim and I take the two children for a swim. This afternoon was really funny. We were drying the two little ones after their swim. I had Emma and Jim was drying Simon. Suddenly Emma says, 'I want a penis like Simon. Why haven't I got a penis?'

'Because you're a little girl,' I said.

'Why can't girls have a penis? I want a penis.' She was shouting this on the beach and everyone was laughing at her.

Jim said, 'You have something else called a vagina. That's how we knew you were a little girl when you were born.'

'Well, I don't want to have a vagina, I want to be like Simon.'

'Well, little girls are made differently from little boys because when they grow up little boys become fathers like me and little girls become mothers like Mummy.'

'I want to be a father like you,' she said, sticking to her point.

'Well then,' said Jim, 'you wouldn't be my little girl, would you? And you couldn't be pretty like Mummy and have a new baby, could you?'

This seemed to settle the argument.

Writing this down has made me think. I've never really thought about these differences between boys and girls. Of course I know we are different and I've seen Neil and Dad around the house when they're dressing and know what they look like. But I've never actually sat and thought about why, and yet here was Emma asking about why—and she's only three!

Suddenly I have realised that the big difference seems to be that everything that makes me a girl is built inside me, hidden away, and everything about a boy that makes him a boy is on the outside: you can see and touch all these parts. I must find out more about boys and how they work—what a lot there is still to learn!

ALL ABOUT BOYS

What Kate wants to know now is probably what you also want to know. Why is a man like he is, and how do all these parts of him work? Does he have any kind of monthly 'period'? What is his share in having babies?

I expect, like Kate, you have noticed that boys and men have quite different sexual organs from girls and women. You have probably seen baby boys having a nappy change, or toddlers and young boys having a 'wee' in the toilet or out

in the country somewhere, sheltered by a tree. Apart from realising that they can stand up for this and girls sit down, you probably have not given it any more thought than Kate did. Look carefully at the picture of the little boy.

You will see in front of his body at the base of the stomach what are called the 'male organs'. They are the *penis* and the *testicles*. More strange names.

Because the names are strange and foreign, small boys often give 'nicknames' to these parts of their body and you hear parents using expressions like 'little willy' and 'wee wee' or 'little tap'. They express the use the child sees for this organ and also make it feel more personal and special to him than some strange foreign word.

It is interesting to see how these 'outside' parts of a boy, or man, link up with his inside so here is another diagram to show you how the parts inside are placed and named.

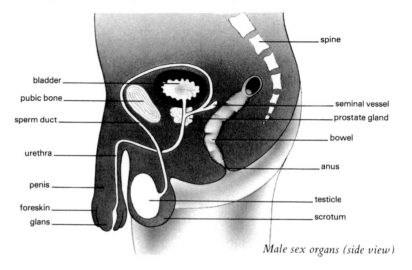

Male sex organs (side view)

You see on the left the pubic bone and on the right the spine, and between them is the urethra or 'canal' for urine (the waste water that is passed through the body) and also the bowel for waste matter.

Most of the sexual organs are clearly on the outside of the man and they are, as you have already seen, the penis and the testicles. What do they do?

If you look again at the diagram you will see that the canal for passing urine continues along the length of the penis. This is the means by which a man passes water outside his body—it corresponds with the urethra you saw in the diagram of a woman.

But it has another important job to do. It is by the penis (through the same canal) that a man can send out his sperm. Sperm is a shortened word for *spermatozoon* (plural *spermatozoa*). This is another strange foreign word: it is the name for the man's 'life-cell'.

This is the share a man has in making new life. He makes

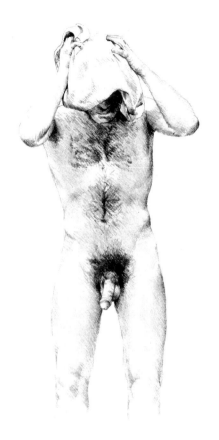

the cell which, when it joins with the woman's ovum (egg), will fertilise the egg and make a baby—a new life.

The testicles are like two little marbles ('balls', most boys call them) contained in a loose skin like a sack which hangs just behind the penis and is called the *scrotum*—not very obvious in a small boy because they are not fully developed. As the boy grows into a man so they grow and drop down into the sack and prepare for his future role of father—like the preparation going on inside you to become a mother.

The testicles are also the sexual glands—you remember reading about your sexual glands called the ovaries, and how they produce certain hormones?

The male sexual glands also produce hormones which give the man his special 'male' characteristics—the deep voice, the hair on his chest, a beard on his chin, strong muscles, broad shoulders. Take a good look at your father or any man you know well, and see how obviously different they are from women. The hormone which does this is called *testosterone*.

So there are two functions for the testicles of a man; to make him virile—manly—and to make the seeds for new life which enable him to become a father.

Whereas in a woman only one egg is produced each month, in a man the testicles are constantly making millions of 'sperm'. They are so tiny that they can only be seen under a microscope—you could put millions into a thimble!

Sperm (magnified)

When they are made they stay in the testicles or pass into the sperm duct (or tube)—the channel that connects the testicles to the urethra, the canal for passing water (see the diagram on page 28 again).

To make it easy for the sperm to pass out of the penis a liquid called semen is made in the seminal vessel (see diagram on page 28). This is a thin milky-looking fluid in which the sperm can swim. You will see from the diagram that the sperm join up with the semen on the way to the penis.

A young man will need to pass the sperm out of his body when he has too many stored in his testicles. Because he is not able to live the life of an adult man, he needs to have a way of getting rid of the unwanted sperm just as a woman has a way of discarding the unwanted egg each month.

This happens to a boy or young man while he is sleeping, and he wakes to find the sticky fluid on his pyjamas. Losing this fluid happens in a moment: it does not go on for several days like a woman's 'period', neither does it happen at regular intervals. It is all over and finished with instantly. When this happens it is called a 'nocturnal emission'; most boys call it a 'wet dream' because that's exactly how it seems to them.

— 4 —

MONDAY

Back to school for the autumn term and I'm really fed up. The summer holidays seem to have changed everyone. The group I belonged to has broken up and we've made new friends with other people. Well, most of them have. I don't seem to have anyone in particular for a friend. The others seem to have met in the holidays and now they talk and laugh about things they did together and I feel left out.

Sometimes I want to be one of them and wish I shared their jokes. Then I get angry—or hurt, it's all the same—and say 'catty' things to them. I really get quite mean and do things I know are wrong. Then again sometimes I feel so grown-up that they all seem childish. Then I want to go off on my own with all this new knowledge like a big secret inside me that I can't properly explain and yet I feel excited about it.

A new girl, Joanne, has joined our form from another school. She seems quite clever, she is pretty and a bit on the plump side (like me!) Some of the girls are already whispering about her and calling her nicknames. Mum says they are probably jealous and anxious that she may turn out cleverer than them. She suggested I might ask her round one evening for tea.

Mum is good at picking up my moods. She seems to know about how I feel without asking questions. I've made up my mind to get my hair cut. There's going to be a new me! I shall have it styled and blow-dried, and Dad's going to buy me a new dress . . .

THURSDAY WEEK

Well, at least the new hairstyle worked: everyone at school noticed, even some of the teachers said it was nice. We are all quite friendly again in our group. I suppose that's because the holidays are farther away now and we see each other every day.

At lunch time today I told Liza about Sarah's baby. Liza is my best friend at school. We started in Infants together and we've always been

friends. We liked the same games and read the same books, and shared lots of things. Just lately I've found I can talk about real things with Liza. I mean not just about lessons and television, but really serious things like growing up, and our families and boys. When I have a row at home I can tell Liza and then I feel better. She only has a mother at home — I think her father left home when she was quite young. She doesn't talk about it, but when she comes round to our place Dad is specially nice to her and she likes it when he calls her his 'number two' daughter.

There seem to be two kinds of friends. Some are just nice to meet and talk and laugh with about ordinary things, but I wouldn't tell them everything or even share my ideas or real feelings about 'life'. Then you get a friend like Liza and you are quite safe to say what you like. I just know I can trust her, and she doesn't go spreading it all around. I think it's because we are honest with each other. Perhaps real friendship means you must be honest. I mean, it's no good pretending with someone: it never lasts. I told Liza about Joanne and we decided we would try to be more friendly with her.

I've seen girls at school who want to get 'in' with a set and they are always pretending they like the same things as the others or they are afraid to be different from the group. In the end they do anything just to be one of them. Then if something happens in school and the group gets into trouble, the girl wishes she wasn't involved because they are not really her friends and she doesn't want to share their troubles—then she ends up with no friends. Joanne isn't like that, she seems too shy to push her way into any group, but she also seems very lonely and anxious to make friends. I notice she brings extra 'goodies' in her lunch box, and offers them around. It won't work, it never does, but how to tell her this? You can't buy friendship, it has to come naturally. You've got to like someone enough to share their troubles as well as their laughs. At any rate that's how it is with Liza and me.

LEARNING ABOUT FRIENDSHIPS

Friends, at this time in your life, fill all kinds of needs for you. They are important, because they help you to know yourself; and, when you need, to forget yourself.

According to which part of you has the greatest need at any time, so you choose your friends. You may feel in need of sympathy and understanding, and will feel drawn towards older girls, or even towards teachers, or friends of your parents. Then you may change to a more secure position where you want to use your own gifts of sympathy and encouragement; and so you will now be moved towards timid, shy people, whom you can help by your friendship. As these two needs in you become more balanced, you will find yourself making friends with young people who share your interests or who give you new interests. These friends often stay with you all your life.

Many people have formed real and lasting friendships at this age, which have grown into deep affection with time. These may well be thought of as successful relationships.

The success of these relationships comes from the amount of 'give and take' that exists in them. Since a relationship involves two people, it will depend on each person working equally at it so that the two personalities fit together.

One of the values that is very necessary for friendship is honesty. It is essential in any good relationship. It is less obvious in the parent-and-you relationship, because living together shows us as we are to others—honesty is almost forced upon us. With friends, it is not the same. We can be any kind of person we want. But although we may do this at first, to impress or to attract, to mystify or to interest, in the end the real 'you' must be allowed to know the real friend, and vice versa, since you are both playing the same game. If not, the friendship will not last.

When you think back about your friendships that are now ended, you can perhaps remember some of the reasons why they ended. You thought that she liked you, but she only 'used' you when there was no one else around. She pretended to like the same things as you, but she became bored with them. She was always nice to you, but when you went to her home, she was horrible to her family. She said nice things about you to yourself, but she talked about you to other people behind your back. For all these reasons, or one, or some, you lost trust in her as a friend. They all add up to dishonesty.

But of course all these things might apply to you as well, and friends may have 'fallen out' with you for similar reasons. . . .

It is not that we mean to be dishonest with our friends. It is all part of the exploring and experiencing of relationships, which we are enjoying (or suffering) at this age. Most young people begin a new relationship by 'playing a part', for most of the reasons mentioned above, but, eventually, you must get to the truth of *who you are*, if the friendship is to last.

In this friendship you want to find a place to relax, where you can be 'you'. You want to find in it someone with whom you can be funny, or silly, or even fed up, someone who will share your jokes, or your secrets, or your ambitions, someone you can argue with, disagree with—and still like.

But if this is what you expect to get from the friendship, then it is also exactly what you must put into it yourself, since, as we have already shown, it depends on both people trying equally hard to be a 'good' friend.

— 5 —

TUESDAY

Today the girls had a talk from the school nurse. She told us all over again about periods. Most of us knew about them, but still it was worth hearing in school because now we know that we all know and that enables us to talk about it if we want to. Not that there's much to say, but if one of us starts her periods she likes to tell someone else in her group.

The nurse showed us different kinds of sanitary pads and how to attach them. One of the girls asked her why she didn't show us tampons, and some of the girls wanted to know what they were. She explained all this and gave us a lecture in hygiene. The P.E. staff are always on about this too.

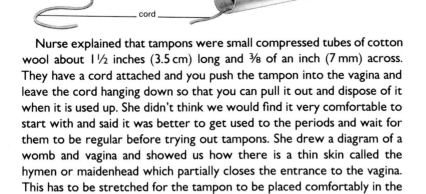

absorbent material

cardboard dispenser

cord

Nurse explained that tampons were small compressed tubes of cotton wool about 1½ inches (3.5 cm) long and ⅜ of an inch (7 mm) across. They have a cord attached and you push the tampon into the vagina and leave the cord hanging down so that you can pull it out and dispose of it when it is used up. She didn't think we would find it very comfortable to start with and said it was better to get used to the periods and wait for them to be regular before trying out tampons. She drew a diagram of a womb and vagina and showed us how there is a thin skin called the hymen or maidenhead which partially closes the entrance to the vagina. This has to be stretched for the tampon to be placed comfortably in the passage. Some girls break this skin through doing energetic sports and it is quite easy for them to use tampons. For others it may be too difficult to break the skin and then the girl would be uncomfortable and miserable trying to put in the tampon. So, her advice was—use pads.

HYGIENE

We have already spoken about the changes that come about through the glands. You may already notice that hair is beginning to grow around the vagina; this is called 'pubic' hair; and also some hair will begin to grow under the arm-pits. With the growth of this hair comes a growth in sweat glands and you will find that you perspire much more than you used to. Usually this is around the armpits, but it may be across your forehead and around your nose and mouth when you are nervous and embarrassed.

Unfortunately, stale perspiration gives off an unpleasant odour which gets into our clothes. Often this is strongest during the few days of menstruation. We've got to pay attention to this and do something to keep ourselves fresh and pretty. The best thing is to bath frequently, every day if possible, but if not, at least to wash all those parts we have mentioned thoroughly each day or more often if necessary. Then we can 'spoil' ourselves with nice talc and some of those deodorants that we see advertised. Try different ones until you find what suits you best; some skins are more sensitive than others to the chemicals used. Ask your mother what she likes using and I'm sure she'll buy you some.

Your skin, too, may become greasy and sometimes spots or blackheads appear. To avoid these the answer is soap, warm water and a clean flannel. Wash your face gently; don't scrub it up and down or you will injure the delicate pores even more.

As important as soap and water is sleep. In sleep your skin relaxes and the creases are smoothed out—sleep is a great beautifier.

Then you want to keep an eye on the things you eat. Try fewer sweets and more green vegetables, fewer crisps and more salads and fruit.

Walk briskly, stand tall, and see how your eyes sparkle and your skin glows.

The happiness of knowing yourself is beginning. The need to love and be loved is growing in you at the same time. You are beginning to feel proud of your appearance.

— 6 —

WEDNESDAY

Well, after all this preparation, at last it has happened. Today was the great day. I discovered I had started during the afternoon break and told Liza. She said I should wait till I got home since it was not worth going to the teacher so late in the day; it would be all right for a little while. She began a few months ago so she knew what it was like.

I couldn't wait to tell Mum. I do believe she knew from my face before I even said a word! She gave me a hug and asked if I was happy about it all and did I have any more questions or did I understand all about it. She must have told Dad because he kept giving me winks and 'special' looks and making little jokes about me wanting a raise in pocket money to celebrate my new status of womanhood. Neil got quite cross about this 'secret' we seemed to be having without him. Well, he'll find out one day.

After all that excitement it was rather an anti-climax, because it just fizzled out after three days. Mum said that was quite normal and it would take a few months to settle into a 'proper routine', as she put it.

MORE ABOUT HAPPINESS

We began this book with Kate thinking about what makes her happy. Just at the moment she is feeling very happy because she feels close to her parents and loved by them.

This is a very important kind of happiness to know about because we learn in this way how to give love to other people and, some day, to our own children.

You could make a long list of all the things happiness is: hopefully one of those things would be family love.

The love of people in a family for one another is very special. It does not always need to be said in words: it shows itself in all kinds of ways. If you spend a little time looking at

families on holiday or enjoying some time together, you will see how they look at each other, how close they sometimes stand, how they touch one another.

Girls will often link their arms through those of mother or father, boys like to punch and tussle with their father in a playful fight—like young lion cubs. Even a teenage boy will square up to his dad in a boxing attitude, whereas a girl will curl into the arm or shoulder of her dad, while mother's arms are often held wide open to catch all who come to her.

These physical contacts belong to people who 'belong' to each other. It would not be appropriate or the right thing to do if you behaved like this with everyone. For instance, you would not want to stand so close to people you do not know —you feel this even when you are too small to understand.

See how a little child will draw away from you and turn to his or her mother if you come too close. We have to build up a trustful and loving relationship with people before we come close, or, as Kate says, share our real feelings honestly.

Sometimes we are confused because people we know and trust suddenly feel too close to us. Their affectionate touches and embraces are no longer comfortable. Our instinct warns us that something is wrong.

We all have a need to keep a little distance between us and others. This is our space in which we find privacy. If anyone gets inside that space uninvited, they are taking advantage of us, abusing us. We must always be aware of our space and guard it constantly. Sometimes the people we are not comfortable with are part of our family circle and we cannot avoid them. Usually you know if the touches feel good or bad. If they feel bad you must say 'No!' If it continues you should tell someone you trust, a teacher or grown-up that you know well. If you can't do any of these things there is ChildLine, which is a phone number you can ring for help. They are people who understand what you are telling them and will advise you what to do. It's not just young children these things happen to. It could happen to friends of Kate or even older girls. Maybe she has a friend walking round with this awful secret and needing someone to talk to. Kate will know how to help her—so do you now.

A loving family is the natural result of a loving marriage. A man and woman who decide to marry have to have a special love for each other. This love begins when they first make friends and grows until they are sure it will last for ever. Then they make the decision to marry and the love goes on growing and getting deeper with more and more understanding as they live together.

All your efforts to make friends and keep them, all the little hurts you get when friendships break up—these are all practices for the future. They are a kind of school in relationships in which you learn about the great love you will need for being a wife and mother.

= 7 =

MONDAY

I am writing this at Sarah's house because it is half-term and I have a whole week to spend here.

I felt quite important having to pack a little bag of S.T.s in my case and hoped she would notice when I unpacked. Of course she did and we had a laugh about the obvious way I showed her. She said it was one of the bonuses about being pregnant that she didn't have to bother with

periods for nine months. I hadn't thought of that! It's only logical when you think about it—if having a period disposes of the lining that has grown in the womb, then when the egg is fertilised and becomes a new life it will need the lining in the womb for a 'bed' and so there will be no more periods until the baby is born.

'But,' I said to Sarah, 'what happens to the other eggs during that time?' Sarah says it all stops. Once again the glands send their messages and no more eggs travel into the womb. That's how a woman knows she is pregnant.

'If your periods stop, does it always mean you are pregnant?' I asked.

'No,' said Sarah. 'Sometimes they stop because a woman is ill or because she is taking certain kinds of pills which can cause the periods to stop. With young girls their periods may stop if they are doing too much slimming and their body weight drops below what is right for them. I hope you haven't any ideas about slimming? Lots of girls your age put on weight, but as long as you eat sensible food your figure will eventually settle into the right shape for you.'

'I know, Mum's always nagging me about eating crisps and chocolate. There's this girl at school who's a bit on the plump side and some of the girls call her "fatty" and make jokes about her when she's near enough to hear. That's what really starts you worrying—what people say to you.'

'Well, I think you are lovely just the way you are,' said Sarah giving me a little hug.

'But if there are so many reasons for periods stopping, what would make you think you were pregnant?'

'Well, to begin with, a woman usually knows if she is likely to become pregnant. After all if you want to have a baby it's a very important decision that two people make, the father and the mother. So naturally you are expecting your periods to stop. Then you can go to the doctor and he or she can tell by examination. The doctor can also do a test of your urine and that will show if you are pregnant. You can also buy do-it-yourself kits from the chemist and do the test at home.'

I understand all that, but what I would really like to understand is how the egg gets fertilised. If a baby has to have a father and a mother, how does the sperm get into the egg?

MAKING A LIFE TOGETHER

You have already read how friendships grow and become more loving the longer they last.

Every good friend you have is a lesson in love. When a boy and girl meet for the first time, they are often shy and a little awkward, and stand apart to talk to one another. When they part, it is with a nod of the head or a little wave of the hand.

Now see how much more friendly and at ease they become after a few meetings. They like each other, they may even hold hands or just stand close and look into each other's face when talking.

Have you noticed a boy and girl in love? Even the word 'couple' joins them together as one unit. They see only each other when they meet. They walk very close, their arms around each other. They offer their lips to each other to kiss. Already they begin to say 'I love you' with their bodies as well as with their words.

Soon they want to be together more and more. They plan their lives together. Meeting is not enough for them. They want to give themselves absolutely to each other for the rest of their lives. They will build all their future together.

When they feel like this they are ready for marriage. They will leave their parents' homes and make their own home together, to become a little unit of their own. In their own home they will learn to love and help one another, to be patient and understanding and forgiving, not being afraid of arguments, but glad to make friends again afterwards.

They will learn to love one another in the special way that is designed for a man and a woman. You have already seen how the sexual parts of a man are outside and a woman's are inside. You can see from the two diagrams printed earlier (on pages 12 and 28) that they fit like two pieces of a jigsaw that come together to make the right picture.

Because of this closeness we like to feel with people we love, a man and a woman love to feel each other's body close against their own, skin touching skin, and the man puts his penis into the vagina of the woman and this is as close as they can be—joined almost like one person.

This is why we talk about people 'making love'. This is what they are doing, loving one another and making more love. Another word you hear used is 'intercourse'. That's a kind of clinical word. A doctor for instance might ask you if you have had 'sexual intercourse'. This is what he or she is talking about, but people in love like a husband and wife would talk about making love rather than having intercourse.

They enjoy this experience very much; sexual love is one of the great pleasures built into our bodies. The human race is intended to continue and the only way for this to happen is for people to have babies. The only sure way to do this is to

45

make the creation of life such a pleasurable thing that men and women want to make love.

All the parts of our bodies that are concerned with sex and the making of babies become involved and alive and sensitive to each other's touch, and this awakens the need in a man and a woman to embrace each other and complete the union of two persons in one great feeling and showing of love.

It is not easy when you are young to understand the strength of this love. For example, little Emma puts her arms round her daddy and hugs him so tightly that it screws up her little face with the effort and she says 'I could hug you to pieces'. She is trying to express a great love. When Sarah holds her babies in her arms she presses their cheek to her

cheek and puts her mouth to the tiny chubby hand and says 'I could eat you, you're so lovely'. These are just some ways that people try to show a love that is too great for words. It seems to say, 'I can't get close enough, I want to climb right inside you and be part of you'.

After a little time of living together, our young couple will want to have a baby so that some of this love can overflow and be shared with another person—not just anyone, but a person they have made themselves out of their love for one another.

To see how this comes about you will need to think back to the journey of the ovum (the egg) in the woman and the man's 'sperm' which he passes in a milky fluid through his penis.

Usually, as you know, the penis is a soft fleshy thing which hangs down between a boy's legs. When the boy becomes a young man and starts to produce sperm, his penis also grows larger.

You remember reading how the sex organs become 'alive and sensitive' when touched? How the man and woman feel a need to love one another closely—to be joined? When this happens to the man, his penis becomes stiff and stands upright. This is called an erection. It is only when this happens that he can put it into the vagina of the woman. That is why caressing one another and touching and kissing are all part of the act of making love—it prepares the man and the woman for being joined together. At the same time that they are joined, the man can send his sperm into the vagina of the woman. Thousands of sperm swim by means of a tiny tail, like tadpoles, up into the womb and along the Fallopian tubes.

If the time is right and there is an ovum released in the tubes, one of the sperm will find it and bury itself in the ovum. The ovum is now fertilised and will grow into a baby within the next nine months: we shall see how this happens later on in this book.

It is a very happy time for the husband and wife and they look forward eagerly to the birth of their baby.

— 8 —

THURSDAY

In the end I asked Sarah about the egg getting fertilised. She explained it all to me.

It's hard to imagine it happening to me, but when I see Jim and Sarah together it seems just right. He's so kind and loving with her. When he comes home in the evening she 'lights up' and is so pleased to see him: they seem to have a little moment all to themselves.

Of course they have arguments sometimes. They argued with each other earlier this week. But then afterwards he put his arm around her shoulders and kissed the back of her neck and said, 'Sorry, I was such a bear', and she snuggled up to him and it was all fine again.

Tonight when Jim came home he patted Sarah's tummy and said, 'How's my baby today?' Sarah told him it had been kicking a lot and not giving her much rest.

I said I didn't know you could feel a baby moving about. Sarah said it moves after about sixteen weeks: now she is seven months pregnant and she can feel the little arms and legs going thump. She told me to come and put my hand flat on her stomach. I was amazed: I could actually feel this strong movement. It made the baby seem much more real than just talking about it. I can see now why parents talk to their babies before they are born. They really are very alive.

'I should think it's twins,' said Jim, laughing at my surprise.

'That would be fun—could it be?' I asked.

'Not very likely,' said Jim. 'Twins usually go in families and we don't have any.'

'What makes twins, then?'

'Well, sometimes the ovaries release two eggs at the same time and then if the sperm found both eggs you would have two babies, but they would be quite different little people and they might be one boy and one girl. But if only one egg was fertilised and divided itself into two separate cells then you would have identical twins. Both babies would look just the same and be the same sex!'

That's what I like about Jim. He treats all my questions seriously and tells me just what I want to know. I bet Dad would have told me some joke, like 'it depends which way you get out of bed in the morning'! (Here are two pictures to show you what Jim was explaining to Kate.)

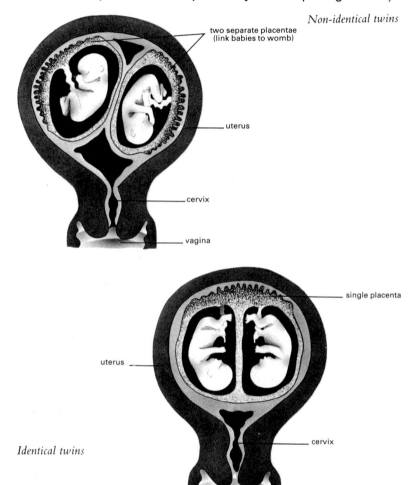

Non-identical twins

two separate placentae
(link babies to womb)

uterus

cervix

vagina

single placenta

uterus

cervix

vagina

Identical twins

SUNDAY

I don't want to go back to school. I wish I could stay with Sarah until the baby comes. I had this sudden thought that something might happen. You always hear grown-ups whispering about things that go wrong.

'What's a "miscarriage", Sarah?' I asked.

'Well, if something went wrong with the baby or some serious accident happened to me, the womb might not be able to carry the baby any more. It would have to try and expel the baby from the womb before the nine months were completed. Sometimes it happens early on in a pregnancy, then the foetus comes away from the wall of the womb with the lining, and passes out through the vagina like a period. Only it would be more serious and much more unpleasant, and you would have to go to bed and rest.

'It's very unlikely. It's not a natural thing to happen so you mustn't worry about things like that. You go regularly to the doctor or a clinic for a check-up and they watch out for anything that might go wrong, and look after you. A friend of mine had a miscarriage and the doctor worked out why and gave her injections and special care the next time and now she has a baby—no problems.'

'So nothing could happen to you after I go home?'

'Good heavens, no! The baby is fine. The doctor at the clinic listens to the heartbeat and feels the head and the shape of the baby, and I can see it moving: everything's all right and you will be the first to know when the baby comes, I promise.'

So that was the end of my half-term with Sarah.

9

WEDNESDAY

I told Liza all about my conversation with Jim and Sarah about the baby. She says I must be the best informed person in the school on the subject of babies!

She thinks Sarah is very lucky having Jim to help her bring up the children. She says it has been hard on her mother all these years doing everything alone and making decisions, and having no one to share her worries.

It's the first time she's ever talked about that to me. I suddenly knew that I really was her best friend. She was really sharing something special with me.

I wished I was Sarah or my mother, I'm sure they'd have found the right thing to say. Instead I just blurted out, 'Your father must have been pretty rotten to leave you all like that.'

Liza said she used to feel like that, so she could understand me saying it. But now she's not so angry. She can see that if two people change so much after they are married that they just make each other's lives miserable, then it's better to separate.

Then she said, 'Besides, it wasn't just that—I've never told this to anyone before, but he had to go because of me.'

'What about you?' I asked, puzzled.

'Well, you know, he used to touch me a lot and try things out with me. It was quite scary in the end so I told my teacher. She was very good to me, and came to talk to my mother. I didn't know how to cope on my own and couldn't bring myself to tell my mother.'

I didn't know what to say. I'd heard about these things happening. I remembered Sarah telling me about loving touches between adults, but this was all wrong. I knew how much Liza must trust me to tell me this, and I wished with all my heart that I could find the right words to say, but nothing came and she went on:

'So you see why I want to be absolutely sure when I marry that it will be the right person—I don't intend getting involved until I'm old enough and sure enough.'

I told all this to Mum in the evening and said that Liza's mum must have been quite glad to end the marriage. But Mum said 'No, it's always sad. No one is ever glad when a marriage breaks up. It is like tearing apart two people who were joined together and both of them get hurt and it takes a long time to heal the wounds—and there is a lot of unhappiness for the children. That is why we should always be kind and loving towards families that are broken up, and try to restore their belief in love and trust and help them to feel wanted again.'

SATURDAY NIGHT

This should have been the best night of the term and instead it has all gone wrong.

We had the school disco and we were all excited and talking about what we would wear. Then Pete said to me, 'See you tonight.' He's hardly talked to me all the term, he grinned at me when I got my hair cut, but that's all, so I was quite excited when he mentioned the disco.

Well, when it came to it, all the girls stayed one side of the room and all the boys the other, and we just looked across at each other. I suppose it was funny in a way, we were all suddenly shy. Then Liza came up to me and said, 'Pete wants to know if you'll walk home with him.' I knew he was watching me and felt myself going red with embarrassment, and I could feel the sweat, and the more I tried not to blush the worse it became, so I just shook my head.

When the disco ended I saw him going out with another girl so I knew I had messed it all up. When I fetched my coat from the cloakroom I saw graffiti all over the walls about Joanne being a 'fatso' and ugly. I was shocked and rushed out to find Liza. We talked about it all the way home. In fact we stood on the corner of the road for so long that I forgot all about the time. I watched Liza walk up her path and then let myself in. Dad was waiting up for me! I've never seen him so angry. He wouldn't even listen to me, just blew his top and sent me to bed—no more discos, no going out next week, no pocket money. I got the whole treatment!

Well, he'll see. He's not the only one who can get angry. I'm not a little girl any more. I'm entitled to some freedom. I don't have to keep telling him where I go. I wish I was Liza, it must be nice not having a father waiting up to tell you off when you've already had a miserable evening. He's just so old-fashioned, he's got no idea what young people are like today.

HOW DO WE BECOME INDEPENDENT?

Let us look at some of the things Kate is saying, because they are what many young people say when they are growing up. Perhaps you have had some of these thoughts.

To begin with, let us get rid of the notion that 'independence' is a declaration of war. Most parents expect independence from you, and want it for you; they know it is necessary, and they have all had to find it themselves. It is really a sign of security. It means you are sure enough of your parents' love to be able to argue with them.

They are always looking out for signs of this 'maturity' developing in you. They want you to be able to make decisions for yourself, to be able to act in a completely unselfish manner. They want you to love them just as they *are*, not for what they have done for you in the past or do for you now.

In the early stages of growing up, you gain the confidence of your parents by showing, in practical ways, your ability to think for yourself. You keep your own room and your own affairs in order. You mend your own clothes and wash and iron personal items of clothing. If you have friends in for the evening, you arrange the meal and you clear away the debris when it is over. You look after the younger members of the family so that your parents can go out together. You would do all these things, I am sure, if you were asked. But offer! It is more adult to offer than to wait to be asked.

Parents don't expect to be loved as a matter of duty nor do they take it for granted. Indeed, many of their attitudes are the result of not being sure that you love them enough to respect their wishes. They give orders and make rules because they are afraid to trust in your love for them. So, if you wish to avoid these 'dictatorship' situations, you must, first and foremost, give them assurance of your love.

They are surprised, delighted, and truly appreciative of everything that you give them, whether it is help or a gift, or just a hug. They have put up with your 'cupboard-love' gladly, when you were little, because of their love for you, but now they need a new kind of love, freely given.

One of the ways to avoid a row with your parents is to tell them, without being asked, where you are going and when you will be back. Any adults living together obey these common courtesies. Husbands and wives do this; students sharing lodgings do this; people living in community do this. So why should you be different?

And if you are young, say whom you are going out with, because this shows that you have nothing to hide. Eventually you will be trusted, without questions, wherever you go.

You have a free will to choose whether you will do the right or wrong thing, but it is also your responsibility to see that what you decide to do will not damage the love possible between you and your parents. That is what being a caring person is all about.

You probably find that it is very difficult to talk about these things with your parents and at the same time to keep cool and calm. You feel angry and upset and misunderstood by them. The more they talk to you the harder it is to be reasonable and you say things you are sorry about.

Afterwards, thinking it over quietly, it is easier to see what they are trying to say and where you may have gone wrong.

Give yourself time to think it out. Go where it is quiet and have a good look at yourself. Never slam shut the door of your mind even if you slam the door of the living room.

Kate is asking for her father to understand her, but she must also try to understand him.

You could make quite a long list of things parents say and what they really mean. Here are just a few examples:

What time do you think this is?	We've been worried and afraid for you.
It's very cold tonight.	You ought to wear a warm coat instead of that little jacket you like so much.
You don't look very well.	You are having too many late nights.
He is quite nice, I suppose.	Your father doesn't trust him and I'm not too keen either.
Run along now and do your homework.	I love you and I've enjoyed talking to you.

The language of love is mysterious. Those who understand it have the secret of life.

— 10 —

CHRISTMAS HOLIDAYS

Sarah has had her baby, a little boy, and everyone is delighted. All the silly angry things we said don't matter anymore. Funny how, when really big things happen, they make all the everyday events seem unimportant. I remember when Grandad died, Mum had just bought me some new shoes and I wanted to wear them for school. I made a stupid fuss because she wouldn't let me. Then in the evening we had the phone call about Grandad and somehow the shoes just weren't important, all we thought about was Grandad. Well, that's how it was when the phone rang. I answered and Jim said 'It's a boy!'

We are going down at the weekend to see them all.

SUNDAY

What fantastic luck! As it's the holidays I'm being allowed to stay and help Sarah. The family has departed, with mum giving all her last-minute instructions: 'Take care of the children—Do what you are told—Don't forget to wash your own things—Help Sarah—Don't go to bed too late, etc.': a funny mixture of 'be responsible' and 'you're still a child'. I'm beginning to wonder if we are always children for our parents and only adults with our own friends.

Anyhow, they've gone, and I know that when I start to get Emma and Simon ready for bed, I shall feel quite different. I don't think about my age any more; I only know what must be done and know that I can do it.

I hope Sarah will tell me all about the baby and how he was born.

Sarah did tell Kate and no doubt you would like to know also, so let us go back a little way to the beginning of this new life.

When the sperm from the father enter the vagina of the

mother, they begin to swim by means of their tails, into the uterus (the womb), and then into the Fallopian tubes.

Here is a picture to show you what is happening.

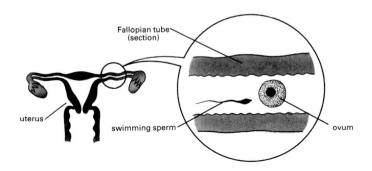

If there is no ovum in the tube, the sperm die. But if they meet an ovum on its way down to the womb, the strongest of the sperm will force its way into the ovum and they become one cell. At that moment, a new life is begun: a baby has begun its journey into this world.

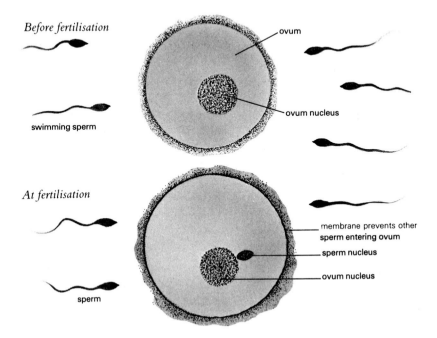

59

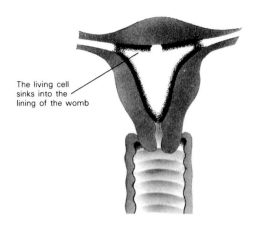

The living cell sinks into the lining of the womb

Right from this moment, certain characteristics of the mother and the father are passed on to the child: things like the colour of eyes and hair, and whether the child will eventually be tall or small. These are 'inherited' characteristics.

At the same time the baby develops its own individual characteristics which will make him or her a unique person, different from all other persons. And the sex of the child is decided, that is, whether the baby will be a boy or a girl.

You already know that a baby grows for nine months inside the mother's body before it is ready to be born. When the ovum and sperm join together the ovum becomes fertilised. (You read that word first when you read the chapter about periods.) This is what the word 'fertilised' means – a living cell made from the joining of a sperm and an ovum.

The living cell is very, very small indeed; you cannot see it or feel it. Within a week or ten days this cell will have arrived in the womb.

You will remember also, from the same chapter about periods, that the womb is preparing itself at this time with a special lining. This lining, you recall, comes away when the ovum is not fertilised.

This time, however, the ovum is fertilised, and so it attaches itself to the lining in the womb and starts to grow. There is no period now for the mother. See how Sarah explained this to Kate during the half-term holiday.

After only four weeks in the womb, the ovum is completely changed. It loses the 'round' look and begins to have a shape that will soon become a 'baby' shape. It is called an 'embryo'.

The next diagram shows you an embryo after six weeks in the womb.

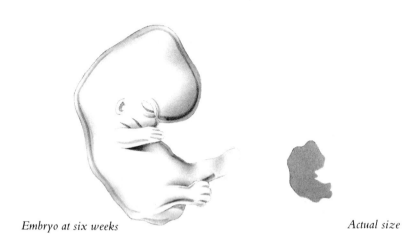

Embryo at six weeks   *Actual size*

The placenta This is very important to the life of the baby. Before a baby is born, his stomach, lungs and bowels do not work as they will after he is born. The placenta does the work of all those organs. It supplies the baby with nourishment and oxygen and gets rid of waste.

It does this by means of the *umbilical cord*. This cord (see the diagram on page 63) joins the baby to the placenta. It is joined to the baby at the navel. That is the little round 'button' we all have in the middle of our stomachs.

The cord is really two tubes, one carrying fresh blood, with all its nourishment, to the baby, and the other tube carrying the stale blood away from the baby.

At the start of the baby's growth, this placenta goes all round the inside of the womb. Inside this placenta is a fluid in which the embryo floats. It is a warm, gentle way of rocking the baby, and at the same time it protects the baby from any bumps or jolts, and enables him to move without hurting himself.

How can the womb contain all these things as well as a growing baby? The womb is a large 'elastic' kind of muscle which can stretch and grow and shape itself around the growing baby.

.After three or four months in the womb, we no longer call the baby an embryo: because it has much more shape and visible features it is called a *foetus* (pronounced feet-us).

The foetus in the womb at 3 months old

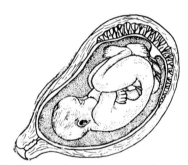

The foetus in the womb at 6 months old

These two diagrams show you how the foetus looks at three months and then at six months. You can see how clearly they look like a baby. You can see on the next page the position that the baby likes to be inside the womb. Sometimes he will turn over with his head downwards, but he doesn't feel uncomfortable that way (as we would!) because of the gentle fluid that rocks him.

At five months he is like any new-born baby to look at, complete with every detail of hair and fingernails, but he is not yet ready to be born. The organs inside him need to develop until they are able to keep him alive outside his mother's womb. He moves his arms and legs about and delights his mother with these reminders of his presence already in the family.

When all his growing is complete he is ready to be born. To do this he gets himself into the best position, which is with his head downwards pressing against the neck of the uterus. When the time comes, the womb will move like a muscle, hardening and relaxing alternately to push the baby out into the vagina and through this to the outside world.

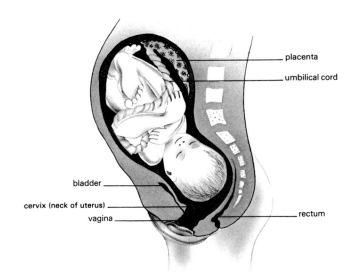

placenta

umbilical cord

bladder

cervix (neck of uterus)

vagina

rectum

The baby is ready to be born

All these parts of a woman's body are made so that they can stretch and open and let the baby through. Afterwards they close up again and become small and firm just as before.

When the mother feels the womb 'contracting' (these are strong, pushing movements) she knows that it is time for the baby to be born. She will go to a maternity home, or perhaps stay in her own home, in bed. A midwife will help her during the time of birth. (The midwife is a nurse specially trained in helping with the birth of babies, known as 'delivering' the baby.)

As soon as the baby appears the mother is told whether it is a boy or girl. The next thing she hears is the wail of the baby as it takes in its first gulp of fresh air.

It is quite usual nowadays for fathers to be invited to stay for the birth of the baby. It is a great encouragement to the mother to have her husband with her and they can share the moment of joy when their baby is born.

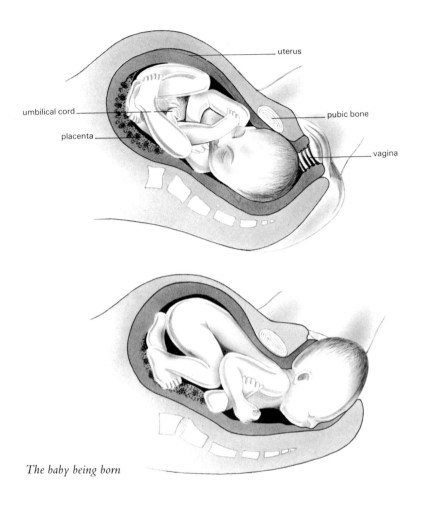

The baby being born

The wonderful thing about this way in which we are born is that it belongs exclusively to human beings. You may have watched films of or even seen animals being born, but there is a great difference about the whole event.

Human beings are the only living creatures who can know how a baby is born, who can choose to live together as husband and wife, and who can plan to have children.

So each time a baby is born there is a complete involvement and awareness of achievement by everyone concerned —the mother, the father and the midwife or doctor.

— || —

MONDAY

The midwife called in today to see if Sarah is all right and to make sure the baby is feeding properly.

I felt very important showing her into the room and holding the little ones quietly while she talked to Sarah. When she left she said Sarah was

very lucky to have such a grown-up niece and told me to make sure Sarah puts her feet up for a rest in the day, and drinks plenty of water.

When she was gone I asked Sarah why she needed to drink. She said it helps the milk to come into the breast.

'How do you make it come when the baby is born and not at other times?' I asked.

'It's all to do with hormones,' Sarah said. 'It's really quite an amazement to me, as soon as the baby is born, there go the glands sending out their messages once more and releasing the right hormones and milk just fills all the little ducts into the breast. You can actually feel the warmth of it as it flows in and swells the breast. Even more amazing is that the baby just knows how to suck. He just snuggles up and drinks as though he had always been used to it.'

'Another thing,' I said. 'The midwife looked at the baby's tummy and lifted the plaster on his navel. I meant to ask you about that before.'

The midwife cuts the umbilical cord

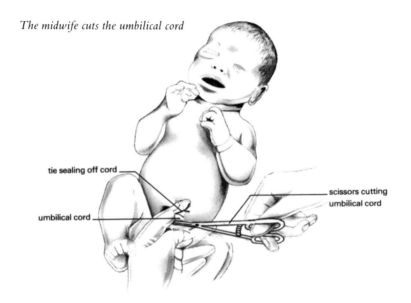

tie sealing off cord

umbilical cord

scissors cutting umbilical cord

AFTER THE BABY IS BORN

Sarah explained to Kate that when the baby is born he is still attached to the umbilical cord—look back if you have forgotten what this is—and this is attached to the placenta still inside the womb. Immediately after the birth, the midwife ties the cord near the baby's stomach and then cuts him free from the cord just above the tied place. This does not hurt the baby; in fact, he cannot feel it at all because the cord is not part of him and is no longer needed. In a few days it shrivels up and comes away like dead skin and all that remains is the little round mark we have called a navel or 'tummy button'. This is what the nurse was checking, ensuring that it was nicely healed and dry.

A few minutes after the birth of the baby, the placenta separates from the womb and comes out through the vagina with some blood. For a few days afterwards the womb will lose a little blood just as it does in a period. After that it begins to return to normal, becoming smaller and firmer. Normal periods do not start straight away. It takes quite a few weeks or even months for everything to return to its normal 'routine'. The mother does not worry about that: she is happy feeding and nursing her baby and resting whenever she can. It can be a very peaceful, contented time in a woman's life.

— 12 —

TUESDAY

Sitting with Jim and watching Sarah feeding her baby it struck me how much like Jim the baby was. 'How can it be,' I asked them, 'that two people share in making a baby and yet it can turn out looking just like one of the parents and not a bit like the other?'

Jim explained that the *nucleus* of the ovum and the nucleus of the sperm each contain characteristics of the mother and the father.

The nucleus means the central part around which other things grow and collect. So the ovum has some part of the characteristics of the mother, and the sperm has some part of the characteristics of the father. When they combine, these parts fuse together and become all one.

If the parts from the father are more dominant, i.e., stronger, than those of the mother, the baby will look more like the father. Similarly if they are stronger on the mother's side, the baby will be more like the mother. Quite often it is a mixture of both: some characteristics will be stronger from one parent or the other, like colour of hair and eyes, though height and shape of bones may come from the other parent.

Every time a baby is conceived (that is, begins his or her life in the womb) the mixture of these characteristics will vary. That is why the children in a family are all different and yet have some things in common.

As well as their looks, children inherit things like temperament and talents from their parents. What makes them unique is the way in which they, as individuals, will use these inherited qualities. They will each put their own self into the development of their characteristics.

'Did you know,' I asked Jim later, 'that the baby would be a boy?'

'No, we decided right from the beginning not to ask when Sarah had the scan—we wanted to wait for the excitement of finding out when the baby was born.'

Sarah laughed and said, 'Imagine knowing from the beginning that you were carrying a boy when you really wanted a girl! How could you start to love the baby? I always think that those nine months are the time when you grow to love and accept this new little life. It seems a very special time to the parents. It is a very close feeling, hard to explain.'

Jim said 'The Chinese count that time as part of the baby's real life—so when the baby is born he is said to be one year old and his birthdays go on from there.'

'I think that's a really nice idea.'

THURSDAY

When Sarah and I were alone, I asked her about 'having the baby'. I understood all about what happens at the birth, but I really wanted to know what it's *like* to have a baby. Sometimes on television you see films of mothers having a baby—it's nearly always in some awful hut or tent or in the middle of some crisis.

You see all sorts of close-ups of the mother sweating and groaning and it looks awful. So I said all that to Sarah. She agreed that it often looks like that in the films, but said it's all part of the drama to create extra excitement in the story.

'Most normal births,' she said, 'take place in much more peaceful surroundings without any great dramatics. I can't pretend it's painless, but it is a totally different kind of pain from, for instance, a wound or a burn or a broken limb.

'Imagine doing something very difficult—I mean, physically difficult—running or swimming or climbing further than you've ever done before, pushing your whole body so hard that you ache in every muscle; you feel at any moment you will break with the effort, and then suddenly you've

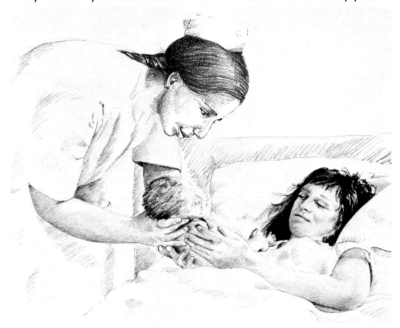

won. You've got up to the top of the mountain, or you've passed the winning line – you sink down exhausted but exhilarated. A marvellous feeling of success and satisfaction and relief and peace fills you completely and every ache is forgotten in the moment of triumph. Well, that's the best way I can describe giving birth: just very hard work for a little while and then it's all over.'

'I've heard girls say they would be scared to have a baby.'

Sarah replied, 'People are only scared of what they don't understand. If you know all about having babies and what is happening to you, there is no need to be scared.

'When you go to the clinic during your pregnancy, they tell you about classes you can attend. Here you can learn how to relax, how to use your muscles and strengthen them, and how to breathe properly. All that makes having the baby much easier.

'When Simon was born I was so busy concentrating on the breathing and counting slowly that I hardly had time to worry about anything else.

'Besides, you can have your husband with you all the time and that's a tremendous help. Somehow you get courage from him just knowing he loves you and how proud he is of you and how he is willing the baby into the world.

'At the moment you are thinking it all out alone, Kate, but one day, when you love someone very much, so much that you want to marry him, you will find how all these things are shared. You are never alone with your fears and worries. You share them all and talk together, and nothing seems impossible when there are two of you.'

= 13 =

Kate returned to her home and school. She had felt very grown up when she was at Sarah's. She had learnt a great deal about marriage and babies. She felt as though married life was just around the corner for her.

However, a few days at school brought her down to earth, and a few reminders from Mum and Dad about getting down to some 'serious work' and 'being her age' made it very obvious that marriage was not 'around the corner'.

Indeed there is still a great deal of 'growing up' to be done before any girl should think of getting married. Having all the facts and knowing about how you develop and how your body works is only a beginning. It is only as you experience the changes in you that you begin to understand the change that happens in your relationships.

Already Kate begins to realise that she can step out of her role of 'child' and behave like an adult, but she is also aware that her parents haven't 'let go' of her as a child and in many ways she knows this is right. It is not yet time. She knows that her friendship with Liza has deepened, but with other girls it has ended. She has discovered that boys grow up as well, that the feelings of friendship between them are different from those she had a year ago. Sometimes she wonders how to find her way in these new relationships. How should she behave? What is expected of her now? How do boys feel about girls?

Perhaps this is just the stage you have reached. These thoughts and uncertainties are all part of adolescence. Everyone, in differing degrees, has been through these moods of worry and impatience. Sometimes you feel angry or frustrated, sometimes you feel low in spirits and 'fed up', sometimes restless and bored. I expect the word 'boring' comes into your talking quite often.

None of this is new and all of it is normal.

You want to be attractive to boys and then you feel a little scared when you have gained their interest.

This desire to be liked by boys is the way we are made. It is called the sex instinct. It is built into our natures so that we will come together and learn to love one another.

It is the way in which you will eventually choose your partner for marriage. Instinct will attract you and then you will find other interests and pleasures in common and after some time you will know that this is a person you could share your life with.

Not everyone gets married, not everyone chooses to be married. People do not have to be married to lead useful lives. Everyone has a choice in this matter. But whether one is married or single, it is still the sexuality built into our natures that will go towards the choice of friends we make and will affect all our relationships with men and women alike.

The very fact that we have a choice is one of the qualities of our human nature. It raises us above all other living creatures. We can use our reason and develop our sense of responsibility until we are able to make a choice—and this applies to everything we do in life. It is the whole purpose of your upbringing—that you should learn how to reason and choose for yourself.

It is a great responsibility to be human. Everything we do reaches out into other people's lives and we have to be continually aware of others and their feelings and their wellbeing.

You must therefore always be aware of how you are behaving with boys, especially when you are in this learning time of your life called adolescence.

If you spend all your time with boys you will miss out on some very good friendships with your own sex. When you have no special boyfriend you may find yourself without girlfriends to go out with because you dropped them all for the boy.

Girls who flirt a lot with boys never make really good friendships with boys. This is because flirting is a kind of act which keeps people away from knowing the real you. It is also concerned with teasing boys into noticing you and not really with caring about the boy.

For a friendship to be a good one, you need to be honest about yourself to others and to yourself. A boy depends on you to be honest, so that he knows how you want him to behave.

You will hear and see all kinds of examples of how boys and girls behave together. You may even feel you are the 'odd one out' who never has any fun. Almost everyone else has these feelings from time to time. This is just another part of growing up. You must be true to yourself. When you have decided for yourself your own standards of behaviour, stay true to them and then both boys and girls will come to respect you because they will know they can trust you.

Being a teenager is not always easy and enjoyable, but is certainly unavoidable. So accept the pleasures along with the difficulties and work all the time towards becoming a lovable person, attractive and desirable as a friend, someone who understands and cares for people.

— 14 —

FRIDAY

Joanne came back to school today. She has been away with flu since the beginning of term. I can't believe how much she has changed—so thin and ill-looking. I asked her if everything was all right with her—she said yes but I thought her eyes filled with tears. This is a job for Mum, I decided, and asked her round for tea.

Mum is great at getting people to talk. Her favourite place is the kitchen. With the excuse of helping with the washing-up, all kinds of confidences are exchanged. A kitchen is such a homely, safe kind of place! Joanne told her all about the nicknames and graffiti and spiteful behaviour going on. She said she had told her mother but begged her not to go to the school, it would only make things worse. She had tried slimming but it had all got out of hand—now she couldn't eat properly.

Mum said she would call round and talk to her mother about what they might do. Meanwhile Joanne should try eating small amounts of food regularly. But she thought it had gone too far for this advice, Joanne would need proper medical and counselling help.

There are times when I could really hug my mother, she has this cool way of taking troubles off my shoulders and dealing with it all herself.

In R.E. we were reading about Abraham and how he wanted a child, but he and his wife didn't have any. That started everyone talking about why people can't have babies.

Miss Medway said quite a number of married people are unable to have babies. She said medical science is discovering a great deal about this and a lot of help can be given to people through the knowledge that doctors have gained in recent years.

We asked her what prevents a person having a baby. She said sometimes it is to do with the woman and sometimes the man. She reminded us of what we had learnt in our biology about the ovum and the sperm. Well, if the womb doesn't grow a proper lining the ovum can't bed itself down when it is fertilised.

Or if the tubes get blocked the ovum can't reach the sperm. Or the man might have a blocked tube or be unable to make the sperm. There are many different reasons, she said, and even just worrying about not being able to have a baby can sometimes prevent it from happening.

'It is always a great sadness to married people if they want children and find they cannot have any. Often they adopt children, which is a very generous thing to do and needs great love and trust in the couple.'

One of the girls said she was adopted and then one or two other people said so were they and suddenly we were all talking about adoption. One thing led to another and the R.E. lesson turned into a lot of questions and everyone talked at once. Miss Medway said obviously we had a lot of things we wanted answers to and she would spend the next few lessons sorting them out with us.

It was Miss Medway, in the end, who sorted out Joanne's troubles. I told Mum about the discussion groups we were having about personal relationships and she told Joanne's mother and they went together to see Miss Medway in the evening.

Everything is much nicer now, everyone is doing their best to help Joanne to settle in. But she is having to go for counselling and some of the girls feel responsible for this—and so they should!

It is often a good thing at this age to talk about these matters to someone sensible, someone you can trust, even when your

parents tell you all you want to know. Some questions only arise out of talking in a group.

Sometimes we don't like to ask questions because we are not sure what our parents will think of us, but when a group of young people talk to a teacher or a counsellor or anyone who takes discussion groups, they can listen to each other's questions and share the answers.

Some things are embarrassing to us during this time of our lives and we prefer to talk to someone not connected with our family. This is not disloyal and does not mean your parents do not understand you. Indeed they understand this very well and would be pleased to think you can get help with your questions in school or from friendly adults.

Many teachers take a great interest in their pupils and remain their form tutor or year teacher all through school. Sometimes the school has a 'counsellor' on the staff; this is another caring person to whom pupils may go. Over the years, all these people collect up many questions from young people and so are able to help them in difficult times.

Here are some of the other questions Kate and her friends discussed in their groups, and some of the answers they thought of. They may help you with your thinking, or they may help you to answer a friend's question.

What is a premature baby?

'Pre' means before and the word 'mature' means fully developed. Premature means a baby born before he is fully developed, that is before the completed nine months in the mother's womb.

When this happens special care is taken of the baby until he is strong enough to manage like a nine-month baby. Sometimes when the baby is very tiny and weak, he is kept in a special incubator. That is a warm, closed-in cradle with glass all round so that the baby can be kept as near to the conditions of his mother's womb and at the same time watched and cared for by the nurses. Usually the mother can take her baby home when he has gained enough weight and is ready to feed like other babies.

What causes this early birth?

Perhaps an illness of the mother, or something happening in the womb, will start the process of birth and the baby pushes his way out into the world too soon. Doctors do not always know exactly why it happens, but they understand a good deal about how to save the baby and care for him until the right time.

It is different from a miscarriage, which you remember Sarah explained to Kate. In a miscarriage the embryo or the foetus dies inside the mother and comes away, whereas the premature baby is very much alive and making his own way into the world. He is just a little too eager and arrives before his proper time.

Why do people have handicapped babies? It doesn't seem fair.

We know quite a lot of reasons why handicapped babies are formed in the womb, but there is much we do not understand.

For instance, some illnesses, like German measles, can affect the baby in the womb. Some drugs used to treat an illness can enter the bloodstream and reach the baby through the placenta.

Alcohol in large quantities and nicotine from cigarettes are two agents which can harm an unborn baby.

It may be that one or other of the minute cells is damaged from the moment the baby begins to grow, so that the handicap is already there from the start.

It doesn't seem fair to us because we have only a human understanding about these things and we would like everything to be perfect. That is a good ideal and one for which all medical research is striving. Every year new discoveries are made and new medicines are developed which correct or modify things which go wrong in the process of a pregnancy.

Of course, a healthy person may become handicapped by illness or accident at any stage in his or her life.

In fact, there are very few people without any handicap of any sort – consider how many wear spectacles or have hear-

ing aids. The greater the handicap, the greater becomes the example of patience and courage. Some people seem to achieve success just because of their handicap. Most families that have a handicapped child will tell you how the child is a focus of love and care for everyone.

Love is very mysterious and works in the strangest ways. People show their very best side when they are working to help someone else; as long as there are handicapped people needing us we have this chance to be our very best selves and also help them to fulfil themselves.

Why do quite young girls have babies when they are not married?

Very often this is just because they are 'quite young'. You already know that menstruation can begin quite early, usually somewhere about twelve or thirteen. You also know that this means the organs of reproduction have started to work and the process is begun in which a baby could begin his life.

All the time you are learning about this you are also learning that your teenage is a preparation time for the more serious task of marriage and looking after a family.

Some young people do not think about this seriously enough—perhaps they do not even think about it at all. They enter into friendships with boys at much too deep a level for their age. Instead of being in control of their own feelings, they let their feelings decide for them what to do.

When a boy and girl are both like this, they may 'find themselves' having sexual intercourse without any real love or sense of responsibility and without thinking just how serious this is. They do not see that it is the great gift we give to the one special person we marry. They have not valued themselves highly enough to think it worth waiting for the right time in their lives.

If this happens at the time that the ovum is in the tube, then the sperm will join with the ovum and a baby is begun.

Whatever brave face a girl may present when this happens, it is only to cover her misery and unhappiness. She is wretched and alone with her feelings, she brings sadness and trouble to her family and her friends. The most loving families will shelter and care for her, but still feel sorrow and regret that it has happened. Being mother or father is no game. It is a very serious commitment that goes with the responsibility of having a home and providing for a new life.

The new life needs both a mother and a father to care for it, not two young people with no future. Often the boy no longer cares for the girl after all this has happened and he will have left her long before the baby is born.

The mother loves her baby and wants to care for him and make up for the loss of a father, but all that doubles the effort she must make. And what happiness is there for her compared with the joy of Sarah and Jim, for example? How can she bear the lonely years of bringing up the baby with no one to share the hopes and fears and pleasures?

She may decide to have the baby adopted, but this is still a heartbreak for her, to part with her own baby and never see him again.

Sometimes it seems as though people don't mind anymore about unmarried mothers. This is not true. It is just that we see more clearly how unfair it is to a baby to reject him because his mother was not married. The baby did not choose this way of arriving into the world, he is innocent of any carelessness. We love and care for him just like any other baby. To do this it is often necessary to help and support the single parent and make her feel loved and wanted so that she can pass this loving warmth on to her baby.

However much loved the mother and the baby are, the community in which they live will still regret the 'incompleteness' of this little family.

Can you only have intercourse when you want a baby?

No. Intercourse is this special way for a man and a woman to love one another. It says 'I love you' in the most loving way possible. Love is endless—when it begins no one says 'I'll love you for a few months, or years!': there is no time limit.

Intercourse is like the seal on the promise of 'for ever'. It says all kinds of loving things to the couple and one of these may be the wish for a baby. When that becomes their intention, they will choose to have intercourse at the most likely time for the ovum to be present in the tubes, hoping that this way the sperm will find and fertilise the egg.

What is a contraceptive?

It is anything used by a couple in sexual intercourse to prevent the sperm meeting the ovum.

The most talked-about one is the pill: you have probably heard or read about it. The woman takes it regularly and it works like the hormone which prevents the ovum from being released into the Fallopian tubes, thus preventing the possibility of pregnancy.

Apart from the pill the most commonly-used contraceptive is a condom. This is a thin rubber sheath which the man uses to cover his penis to prevent sperm entering the womb.

The woman can wear a similar form of protection which covers the entrance to the womb, and there are various other designs and forms of contraception. Family Planning Clinics offer detailed information and advice about the various different methods.

Many people do not wish to use a contraceptive for reasons of health, comfort or religious beliefs—or simply because they *want* to have children. There are ways of recording the monthly period so that the couple can decide for themselves when is the right time to have intercourse if they want a baby and what days to avoid if they do not want a child. A great deal of research has gone into developing this natural method of birth control, and information and help can be obtained from the Natural Family Planning Association.

All these methods have in common the need to plan a family carefully. If every baby is to have its share of loving and caring it must first of all be wanted. At the same time we must remember that our human nature is not a machine or a computer. It is subject to all manner of changes, moods and uncertainties. That is why not every baby in a family may start off as a carefully planned event, but few end up unloved or unwanted.

On the television there is this advert about condoms. First there is a voice saying they had no idea their partner was HIV-positive, and then they say they would have worn a condom if they had known. What's all that about?

Well, we've been talking about condoms already, and you'll know that they are used as contraceptives, to prevent the man's semen getting into the woman's body and making her pregnant.

But nowadays there's another reason why people might want to prevent the man's semen getting into someone else's body, and that is because of the danger of AIDS. AIDS is the condition in which a person's ability to fight infection has been damaged so much by the HIV virus that eventually he or she dies. Although we now have some treatments for the symptoms, no cure has yet been found. So the important thing is to prevent infection with the HIV virus. This is easy to do because the virus can only be passed from one person to another through blood, vaginal fluid or semen. Some people have been infected with the HIV virus by being in contact with someone else's vaginal fluid or semen in sexual inter-course. One way to reduce that risk is by wearing a condom. This protects the woman from the man's semen, and protects the man from the woman's vaginal fluid. So that's the point of the advertisement: to help people to cut down the risk they take when they have sex with someone who may be infected with HIV. But it's important to remember that even con-doms are not completely safe, whether it's pregnancy or HIV the person is trying to avoid.

Many people who have the HIV virus don't know they have it, and there are no symptoms; so there may always be some risk with sex, even with someone you love and trust. We have talked a lot about the way a loving relationship grows, and how we arrive at the stage where we see marriage as the fulfilment of this relationship. Waiting for this time to come is a good way of limiting the risk.

I read in the paper about three brothers in one family who had AIDS. They were only young boys so it couldn't have been from sexual intercourse. Would it be something to do with blood?

Yes. Blood is another body fluid which can pass on HIV infection. Mothers who are HIV-positive can pass it on to their babies through their blood. Before enough was known about AIDS and how to test for it, some people received blood that already contained the virus. Since then the blood from every donor is tested and great care is taken to prevent such a happening. The boys you read about were haemophiliacs and had all received contaminated blood products at some time when they were very young and needed treatment for bleeding. They were given a hard time of it at school and in the end the family had to move. This is a really bad thing to happen. I hope if you ever meet a young person at school or in the neighbourhood who has AIDS, you will give them sympathy and friendship. People with AIDS need all the support you can give. It is not dangerous to kiss, or hug, or touch these people. I expect you've seen pictures on television of famous people showing us that they can safely make physical contact with these sufferers—it is to reassure you as much as for the person concerned.

It is very frightening, at any age, to have a disease from which you know you will die. Try to share some of your own happiness with these people and help them to feel valued. Good relationships are not just about love and marriage. They are about making a happier world in which people can develop and become their best selves.

It is not fair that women should have all the bother of having the pregnancy and a baby, and the man doesn't have to put up with any inconvenience.

This might have been true many years ago, but certainly not today. In every loving family the husband takes his part in the caring and rearing of his children. He loves to be involved right from the start and even shares in the moment of birth. He stays with his wife and encourages her and does all he can to give her strength.

During the pregnancy he helps more in the household and sees that she has plenty of rest. He spoils her with little treats and is especially loving and tender towards her.

The wife on the other hand feels privileged to be carrying their baby and proud of her achievement when the baby is born.

In a loving relationship there is no adding up the score for who does the most.

Some people don't believe in marriage, they just live together.

Getting married is like making a public statement to everyone that you want to be thought of as husband and wife now and forever.

Christians make this statement in a church before God as a witness to their intentions and showing their need of His help.

Some people marry in register offices – they do not consider marriage has a religious meaning, but they do think it is a social matter involving the community. If neither of these ceremonies is considered necessary a couple may just decide to live together. Their commitment may be just as great to one another and the relationship every bit as loving

and permanent—they are to all intents and purposes married although it presents legal and social difficulties in a society where marriage is the normal thing.

But if living together is chosen as a way of avoiding permanent entanglements, as an easy way to become free again, then it is not really a marriage. It is not even an honest relationship because each is saying, 'I will end it when I want to'. They may think it is honest to say this to each other, but they are not honest in pretending that it will not hurt either person when it ends. The ending is always painful and the fear of it ending destroys the nature of love.

What is an abortion?

An abortion is putting an end to a pregnancy and so destroying the new life in the womb.

Sometimes nature makes its own abortion. If the ovum has not been properly fertilised, or the womb is unable to support the new life, it will abort itself and the embryo will come away of its own accord.

However, it is also possible for women to have an abortion by their own choice. Certain doctors and hospitals will agree to bring about this abortion with the use of drugs or by an operation. There are many reasons such as illness, poverty or too many children that may cause a woman to make this decision.

Sometimes she decides alone, sometimes after much thinking and talking with her husband, or with her family or her doctor. It is a sad decision which often has unhappy effects, especially for the woman.

There are many people who think it is very wrong to end a life in the womb. If you look back at the pictures of how a baby grows and lives in the womb, you can see how very real this life is. There is no doubt that the baby at every stage is a living being. Many doctors and nurses refuse to carry out this operation, for they regard it as killing a baby.

Others accept it, believing that the baby does not become a person until it has separate life from the mother.

You will no doubt talk and argue about this many times while you are growing up and even as an adult you may be asked what you think. It is a subject that people feel very strongly about.

Kate has no doubts about what she thinks at present. She has lived with Sarah and Jim and heard them talk to their new baby in the womb. She has felt him move and shared their excitement about every stage of the pregnancy. For her the baby was a real person from the time he began his life in Sarah. It is all a matter of loving and wanting a baby. If you really don't want a baby you must make sure you do not bring a new life into being.

What is a homosexual?

Everything you have read in this book has been about the love a man and woman have for each other, which usually leads to marriage and having children. That is the way most people are made, and the future of the human race depends upon this love.

A homosexual is unable to experience this kind of sexual love for a person of the opposite sex. He or she may only have these feelings about people of the same sex. If we are talking about a woman, we use the word 'lesbian'. There is still a great deal to learn about the reasons why some people are homosexual; people are looking for greater understanding about this.

Homosexuals want to live their own kind of life and to accept themselves as they are. We should accept each one as a person in his or her own right, likeable, lovable and truly human. We must also be truly ourselves in relation to them. That means, for you, be natural and behave as you would towards any friend or acquaintance. A homosexual has as much right to courtesy and respect as a heterosexual—we are all groups in the human family.

Homosexuality is often discussed in magazines and on television. Plays and stories are written to try and understand how it affects people's lives. Some young people, when they see all this, begin to worry about themselves and their own sexuality.

You may be very fond of a particular girl or young woman at the present time: this is perfectly normal. It is part of the natural way that we learn to love. It is part of the process of growing up and falling in love with someone of the opposite sex.

At the age you are now, all your friends, like you, are growing through various stages of loving and learning to love. It is not until boys and girls have matured into men and women that their full sexuality is developed and they become confident about their feelings towards each other. For now, be true to yourself and your own feelings.

What is rape?

Newspapers sometimes report cases of rape and you hear people discussing this with very strong feelings. That is because it is always a violent and hateful crime.

It is forcing a person to have physical sexual intercourse. The word 'forcing' here is the reason for its violence and only very disturbed and unbalanced people would commit such an offence.

Victims of rape are greatly to be pitied because such a thing is not just damaging physically, it seriously damages their feelings and their whole attitude to what should be a loving and happy experience.

That is the main reason for your parents' concern about where you are and who you are with. They love you very dearly and do not want any harm to come to you. They constantly told you since you were very small never to talk to strangers, never to accept a lift in a car, never, if possible, be out walking alone at night. These are still very good rules and you must give serious attention to them. Make sure you come home from discos and parties in groups and always give your parents a time to expect you. It reassures them that you can be trusted and saves unnecessary worry.

— 15 —

TUESDAY

At last the end of term and another disco. I'm really looking forward to this one. Pete stopped me on the way out of school and asked if I was going tonight. When I said 'Yes' he looked pleased and said 'See you there—and this time I want to take you home.' It gave me a funny butterfly feeling in my stomach to be spoken to like that! I hadn't realised how tall and grown-up he had become.

When I was ready to go, I had a good look at myself in the long mirror. I am nearly as tall as Pete now, not a bad figure at all, I was quite pleased with what I saw. I'm not a Miss World, but I felt pretty. When you feel pretty it's surprising how it somehow *makes* you pretty.

When I went downstairs Mum raised her eyebrows and said, 'You'll be breaking all the boys' hearts tonight.'

I thought it was a funny old-fashioned kind of thing to say but I knew it was a compliment so I was pleased.

Then Dad said, 'Hey, who's the lucky boy? I'm jealous.' It really is nice being admired by one's parents!

THE CHRISTENING

What a weekend to remember! First the disco and then being god-mother to Sarah's baby.

Godmothers sometimes have a way of disappearing out of the life of a baby and when he grows up he never knows who his godmother is. I intend to be really special to John (that's going to be his name). I shall try to remember all his birthdays and the big events in his life.

When I stood at the door of the church holding John in my arms, I thought how it might be my baby in a few years' time and how strange it all is. Life just goes on starting again and again.

There's Grandpa there watching his children being mothers and fathers. My parents are watching us grow up and wondering whether we shall become mothers and fathers.

Auntie Felicity didn't marry but she doesn't seem to mind. She always wanted to travel. And that's what she's done. She's a courier in a travel agency and visits hotels and decides if they are good to use. If I chose a career instead of marriage, I thought, that's just how I'd like to be — and have my own flat and car and be independent.

The midwife who visited Sarah was also at the church. She's never been married either. Imagine seeing all those babies into the world and none of your own. Well, perhaps that's a really good way of sharing in other people's happiness. Everyone likes her, she must be a really good person to give her life to nursing.

In fact, I decided, you don't have to get married at all, there are plenty of fulfilling ways of living without marriage. On the other hand . . . oh well, at least I am free to choose. No one can make me get married. Perhaps I shall have the best of two worlds, a career and marriage.

THE END IS THE BEGINNING

This is where we leave Kate. She is a normal happy young adolescent. There are high days when things are great and low days when things are bad for her. She has lots of excitements in store for her and also her share of sorrows.

She has learnt a great deal about herself and about other people in the last year or two. Now she stands at the door of the church and thinks about the future.

This is, in a way, where you stand now. Not at the door of the church, perhaps, but at the door of life. Step forward with courage and confidence — the confidence that comes from knowledge and from being loved.

Real love is learnt, it doesn't just happen. Whenever we give a little time or thought or help to others this love grows in us. We become caring people. That's what good parents are — caring people.